PUBLIC LIBRARY, DISTRICT OF COLUMBIA

W9-ARZ-091

My First Book of
Chinese Words

Published by Tuttle Publishing, an imprint of Periplus Editions (HK) Ltd.

www.tuttlepublishing.com

Copyright © 2013 Text and Illustrations by Periplus Editions (HK) Ltd.
All rights reserved. No part of this publication may be reproduced or utilized in any form or by any means, electronic or mechanical, including photocopying, recording, or by any information storage and retrieval system, without prior written permission from the publisher.

ISBN 978-0-8048-4941-8
(Previously published under ISBN 978-0-8048-4367-6; LCC No. 2012029068)

Distributed by

North America, Latin America & Europe
Tuttle Publishing
364 Innovation Drive
North Clarendon
VT 05759-9436 U.S.A.
Tel: 1 (802) 773-8930
Fax: 1 (802) 773-6993
info@tuttlepublishing.com
www.tuttlepublishing.com

Japan
Tuttle Publishing
Yaekari Building, 3rd Floor
5-4-12 Osaki
Shinagawa-ku, Tokyo 141 0032
Tel: (81) 3 5437-0171
Fax: (81) 3 5437-0755
sales@tuttle.co.jp
www.tuttle.co.jp

Asia Pacific
Berkeley Books Pte. Ltd.
61 Tai Seng Avenue # 02-12
Singapore 534167
Tel: (65) 6280-1330
Fax: (65) 6280-6290
inquiries@periplus.com.sg
www.periplus.com

20 19 18 17   10 9 8 7 6 5 4 3 2 1
Printed in China   1704RR

TUTTLE PUBLISHING® is a registered trademark of Tuttle Publishing, a division of Periplus Editions (HK) Ltd.

ABOUT TUTTLE
"Books to Span the East and West"

Our core mission at Tuttle Publishing is to create books which bring people together one page at a time. Tuttle was founded in 1832 in the small New England town of Rutland, Vermont (USA). Our fundamental values remain as strong today as they were then—to publish best-in-class books informing the English-speaking world about the countries and peoples of Asia. The world has become a smaller place today and Asia's economic, cultural and political influence has expanded, yet the need for meaningful dialogue and information about this diverse region has never been greater. Since 1948, Tuttle has been a leader in publishing books on the cultures, arts, cuisines, languages and literatures of Asia. Our authors and photographers have won numerous awards and Tuttle has published thousands of books on subjects ranging from martial arts to paper crafts. We welcome you to explore the wealth of information available on Asia at www.tuttlepublishing.com.

My First Book of Chinese Words

An ABC Rhyming Book of Chinese Language and Culture

by Faye-Lynn Wu
Illustrated by Aya Padrón

TUTTLE Publishing
Tokyo | Rutland, Vermont | Singapore

Dedication

Thank you to Mimi Gold and Siu-Mui Woo for
their guidance, and my siblings who helped create
the fun for my childhood memories.   F.W.

To Zoe.   A.P.

Preface

Similar to other Roman-based languages, the English language's phonetic and writing systems are tied together. Each letter in a word represents one of its sounds. Unlike English, Chinese writing is a pictographic system that evolved from pictures and symbols. The characters represent words and meanings, but not necessarily the sounds.

The goal of this book is to use playful rhymes and illustrations to introduce the Chinese language to young children. The words covered in this book include objects and actions that children across cultures are familiar with, such as body parts, moon, sun, saying goodbye, and words that specifically relate to the Chinese culture, such as bāozi (a Chinese snack food) and kuàizi (chopsticks).

You will see that each Chinese character is spelled in Pinyin, a phonetic sound system that uses Roman letters to transcribe the Chinese sounds. Pinyin assigns letters different sound values from those of English. For example:

c is pronounced as ts in "its"

ch is pronounced as ch in "chirp"

j is pronounced as j in "jeep"

q is pronounced as ch in "cheap"

x is pronounced as sh in "she"

r is pronounced as z in "azure"

sh is pronounced as sh in "shut"

z is pronounced as ds in " woods"

zh is pronounced as j in "jam"

To hear the Chinese words in this book spoken aloud, please visit this book's page at www.tuttlepublishing.com.

You'll also note that several of the words chosen are written in Traditional as well as Simplified characters.

Although Chinese differs greatly from English, it is a fun language to learn, and young children are ideal learners of new languages. We hope you'll enjoy sharing the Chinese language with your child through these fun rhymes.

simplified | traditional

A is for *ài*,
a word that means love
like the gentle hugs
that wrap us like the
soft wings of a dove.

6

包子

B is for *bāozi.*
A **bun** of soft dough
filled with tasty bits—
when it's hot eat it slow!

Bāozi is a traditional Chinese snack.
It can be filled with meat or veggies,
or with sweet bean paste. Yum!

C is for *chá*,
a steaming cup of tea.
We all sit around the
table, and the cup is
passed from you to me.

Tea is the most common
drink among Chinese
people. It is enjoyed with
meals and snacks, and
also with company.

灯
笼
implified

燈
籠
traditional

D is for *dēnglóng*,
lantern hung up high—
a bright paper lamp
against the night sky.

Lanterns represent joy,
harmony, and good luck.
At Lantern Festival people
like to hang riddles from
them so their friends can
have fun guessing.

猜灯谜

耳

E is for *ěr*.
This is your ear,
listening, listening—
what do you hear?

风
筝
simplified

風
筝
traditional

F is for *fēngzhēng*.
A **kite** soars in the sky
like a beautiful dancer,
swirls, twirls, waves goodbye.

It's said that the Chinese invented kites thousands of years ago!

狗

G is for *gǒu*.
Our **dog** very dear
gives a happy "wang wang!"
when friends come near.

Different people hear and describe
sounds differently. The Chinese
hear cats say *mee mee*, ducks say
gua gua, and cows say *mou mou*.
What do you hear?

12

H is for *hóng*,
the happy color **red**.
We see it all around us
when the new year is ahead.

红 | 紅

simplified | traditional

The color red stands
for happiness.
It is usually used
to decorate when
festivals come
around, like Chinese
New Year and
weddings and many
other celebrations.

冰

I is for ice.
We call it *bīng*.
It's cold in my mouth,
but then soon it's melting.

The letter **i** Chinese sounds like e does in English words like "bee" and "feet." In pinyin, **i** is always followed by a consonant.

家

J is for *jiā.*
My home is my nest,
a place to return to—
that's where I rest.

15

筷子

K is for *kuàizi*, chopsticks—it takes two to bring yummy bites from your plate to you.

16

L is for *lóng*.
Dragon power is good.
With a big, mighty roar
dragon guards our
neighborhood.

龙
simplified

龍
traditional

In Chinese culture the dragon means strength, generosity, and good luck. In Chinese neighborhoods all over the world the dragon dance celebrates happy occasions.

M is for *mǐ*,
a bowl of cooked **rice**,
piled up high,
so steamy and nice.

Rice is a very important dish in
Chinese culture. Some families
like to eat it with every meal.

奶
奶

N is for *năinai*.
Grandmas are sweet.
They give us hugs and love
and, sometimes, a treat.

There are lots
of ways to say
"Grandma" in
Chinese, like *popo*,
yinyin and *ama*.

19

O is for *ōu*.
See how the gull flies.
Circling above,
"o-o I'm hungry!" he cries.

鸥 | 鷗

simplified | traditional

朋
友

P is for *péngyǒu*, the
friends we see each day.
Laughing, holding hands,
together we play.

球

Q is for *qiú*.
A ball smooth and round
bounces high to the sky
and comes back to the ground.

日

R is for *rì*.
The bright, hot sun
with a shining
happy face says
"Get up! It's time
for fun!"

手 S is for *shǒu*.
What can your hands do?
They touch, count,
build, play—and
can tickle, too!

头
simplified

頭
traditional

T is for *tóu*.
Your wonderful **head**
lets you see, hear, smell, taste and talk,
and remember what is said.

雨伞
simplified

雨傘
traditional

U is for umbrella.
When rain falls from the sky
we need our *yǔsǎn*
to keep us dry.

In pinyin the letter u rhymes with the
English word "blue." This letter is
never used at the beginning of a word.

小提琴

V is for **violin**.
We call it *xiǎotíqín*.
Draw the bow over
the strings—
the *xiǎotíqín* sings!

Chinese doesn't have
a v sound but Chinese
culture has lots of
beautiful violin music.

尾
巴

W is for *wěibā*.
A happy wagging tail
greets you with joy
day or night, without fail.

熊
猫

X is for *xióngmāo*.
Furry **panda**, soft as
sheep, munches on
bamboo leaves and
drifts off to sleep.

29

月

Y is for *yuè*.
The moon shines so bright.
Dancing with twinkling stars,
it lights up the dark night.

再见

simplified

再見

traditional

Z is for _zàijiàn._
"Goodbye!" we say—
more good times together
when we meet another day.

Zài 再 means "again" and jiàn 见 means "see."
When the two words are put together they mean
"See you again!" which is how Chinese people
say "goodbye."

List of Words

Ài Love

Bāozi Bun

Chá Tea

Dēnglóng Lantern

Ěr Ear

Fēngzhēng Kite

Gǒu Dog

Hóng Red

Ice (Bīng)

Jiā Home

Kuàizi Chopsticks

Lóng Dragon

Mǐ Rice

Nǎinai Grandma

Ōu Gull

Péngyǒu Friends

Qiú Ball

Rì Sun

Shǒu Hands

Tóu Head

Umbrella (Yǔsǎn)

Violin (Xiǎotíqín)

Wěibā Tail

Xióngmāo Panda

Yuè Moon

Zàijiàn Goodbye